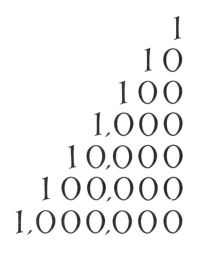

1
10
100
1,000
10,000
100,000
1,000,000

HOW MUCH IS A MILLION?

MARVELOSISSIMO ☆ ☆ THE MATHEMATICAL ☆ MAGICIAN

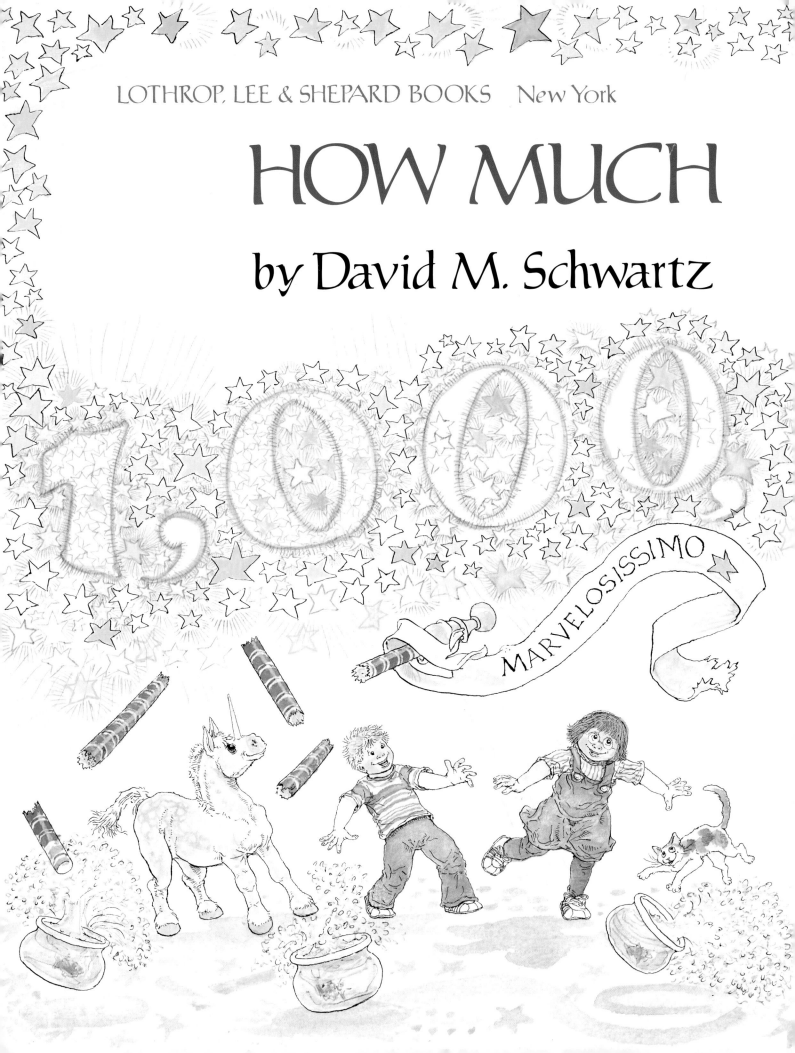

LOTHROP, LEE & SHEPARD BOOKS New York

HOW MUCH

by David M. Schwartz

1,000,000

MARVELOSISSIMO

IS A MILLION?

pictures by Steven Kellogg

THE MATHEMATICAL MAGICIAN

For Mom and Dad, who started
me on the little numbers; for
Judy, who made me pick up the pace;
and for Mary Lou, who is one in a million.
—DMS

To Pam and Steve,
with a million loving wishes.
—SK

Library of Congress Cataloging in Publication Data. Schwartz, David M. How much is a million?
Summary: Text and pictures try to make possible the conceptualization of a million, a billion, and a
trillion.   1. Million (The number)—Juvenile literature.   2. Billion (The number)—Juvenile literature.
3. Trillion (The number)—Juvenile literature.   [1. Million (The number)   2. Billion (The number)
3. Trillion (The number)   4. Number concept]   I. Kellogg, Steven, ill.   II. Title.   QA141.3.S45
1985   513'.2   84-5736
ISBN 0-688-04049-7   ISBN 0-688-04050-0 (lib. bdg.)

MARVELOSISSIMO THE MATHEMATICAL MAGICIAN

IF ONE MILLION KIDS CLIMBED ONTO
ONE ANOTHER'S SHOULDERS, THEY WOULD BE...

TALLER THAN THE
TALLEST BUILDINGS,

HIGHER THAN THE
HIGHEST MOUNTAINS,

AND FARTHER UP THAN AIRPLANES CAN FLY.

IF YOU WANTED TO COUNT FROM ONE TO ONE MILLION . . .

IT WOULD TAKE YOU ABOUT 23 DAYS.

IF A GOLDFISH BOWL WERE BIG ENOUGH
FOR A MILLION GOLDFISH...

IT WOULD BE LARGE ENOUGH TO HOLD A WHALE.

PRESTO! ONE HUNDRED STARS.
IF THIS BOOK HAD A MILLION TINY STARS,
THEY WOULD FILL SEVENTY PAGES. CLIMB ABOARD!

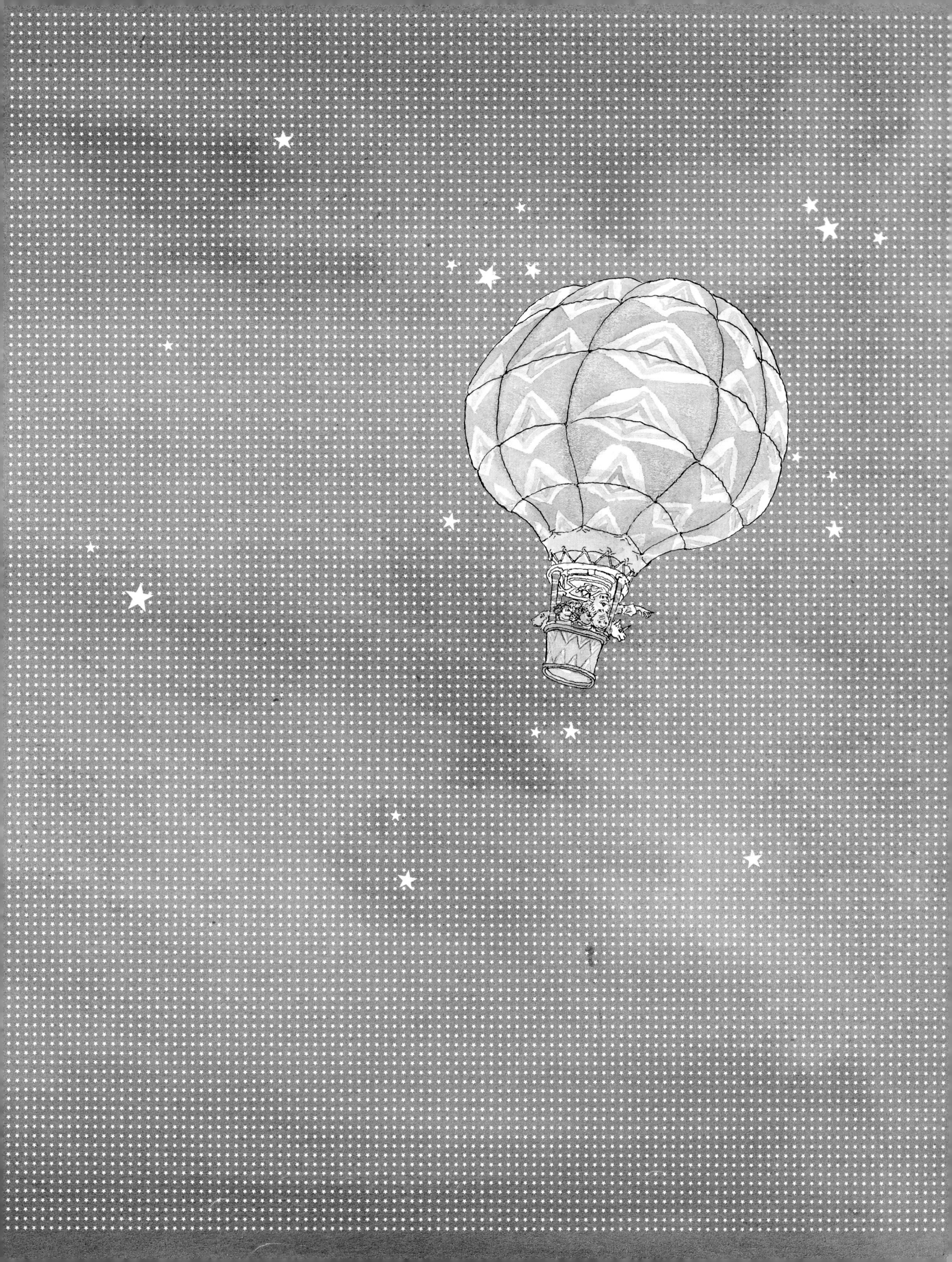

HOW BIG IS A BILLION?

IF A BILLION KIDS MADE A HUMAN TOWER . . .

THEY WOULD STAND UP PAST THE MOON.

IF YOU SAT DOWN TO COUNT FROM ONE TO ONE BILLION . . .

YOU WOULD BE COUNTING FOR 95 YEARS.

IF YOU FOUND A GOLDFISH BOWL LARGE ENOUGH
TO HOLD A BILLION GOLDFISH,
IT WOULD BE AS BIG AS A STADIUM.

IF THIS BOOK HAD A BILLION TINY STARS ...

ITS PAGES SPREAD SIDE BY SIDE
WOULD STRETCH ALMOST TEN MILES.

HOW TREMENDOUS IS A TRILLION?

IF A TRILLION KIDS STOOD ON TOP OF EACH OTHER,
THEY WOULD REACH WAY, WAY, WAY BEYOND THE MOON—

BEYOND MARS AND JUPITER, TOO,
AND ALMOST AS FAR AS SATURN'S RINGS.

IF YOU WANTED TO COUNT FROM ONE TO ONE TRILLION . . .

IT WOULD TAKE YOU ALMOST 200,000 YEARS.

IF YOU PUT A TRILLION GOLDFISH IN A GOLDFISH BOWL...

THE BOWL WOULD HAVE TO BE AS BIG AS A CITY HARBOR.

IF YOU PUT A TRILLION OF OUR STARS
ONTO A GIGANTIC ROLL OF PAPER,
IT WOULD STRETCH ALL THE WAY
FROM NEW YORK TO NEW ZEALAND.

A NOTE FROM THE AUTHOR

For readers who would like to follow the arithmetic journey we've taken with Marvelosissimo, here are the calculations I used. Bear in mind that a million is a thousand thousand; a billion is a thousand million; and a trillion is a thousand billion. Away we go!

TALLER THAN …

Some children are tall and some are short, but 4'8" is an average height for elementary-school pupils. Since the shoulders of a 4'8" child are about four feet high, the height, in feet, of a tower formed by children standing on each other's shoulders would equal four times the number of children involved. Thus, a column consisting of one million kids would be four million feet high, which is approximately 757½ miles. [4,000,000 feet ÷ 5,280 feet per mile = 757.58 miles.] Mt. Everest, the tallest mountain in the world, is 29,028 feet (5½ miles) high. The highest clouds, called cirrus clouds, can go as high as 45,000 feet (9¼ miles). Commercial airplanes flying long distances usually travel 35,000 feet above the ground, and the highest any airplane has ever flown is 86,000 feet (16¼ miles).

One billion of our 4'8" climbers would stand about four billion feet high, which is about the same as 758,000 miles. [4,000,000,000 feet ÷ 5,280 feet per mile = 757,575 miles.] The moon is about 239,000 miles from earth, and so, in fact, this human tower would stand about three times as high as the moon.

One trillion of our 4'8" climbers would stand four trillion feet high, which is a little under 758 million miles. [4,000,000,000,000 feet ÷ 5,280 feet per mile = 757,575,757 miles.] The moon, as we saw before, is about 239 thousand miles from earth. Mars ranges from 35 to 248 million miles away, depending on its place in orbit relative to the earth; Jupiter is 390 to 576 million miles away. Saturn, the ringed planet, is, at its closest, 734 million miles from earth; at its farthest point, Saturn's orbit is more than one billion (1,000 million) miles away. Thus, our imaginary stack of a trillion people would reach Saturn's rings if the planet happened to be at its closest to earth; most of the time, however, the space-kids wouldn't be quite high enough.

IF YOU WANTED TO COUNT …

Most of the numbers between one and one million are long and hard to say. Although the small numbers at the beginning are short, you will quickly move past them and face numbers like 69,828 (sixty-nine thousand, eight hundred twenty-eight) or 711,499 (seven hundred eleven thousand, four hundred ninety-nine). It probably takes you at least two seconds to pronounce long numbers like these. Let's pretend that you started counting from one to one million, that you did not stop to eat or sleep, and that you took two seconds to say each number. There are one million numbers, and so it would take you two million seconds to say them all. Two million seconds is the same as 33,333 minutes, which is the same as 555½ hours, which is the same as approximately 23 days! [2,000,000 seconds ÷ 60 seconds per minute ÷ 60 minutes per hour ÷ 24 hours per day = 23.148 days.]

In counting from one to one billion, you will encounter many, many numbers that take even longer to say than those you met on your way to one million! Try to say, for instance, 98,726,803 (ninety-eight million, seven hundred twenty-six thousand, eight hundred three) or 347,996,268 (three hundred forty-seven million, nine hundred ninety-six thousand, two hundred sixty-eight). How long did it take you to pronounce each of those? If you're fast, you can say numbers that large in three seconds. Actually, if you pronounce all the syllables, it will probably take you a little longer than three seconds, but because some numbers (like 22 or 4,500) are easy to say, let's agree that three seconds is a good average time for the numbers between one and one billion.

So, to count all these numbers (there are a billion of them), it would take you three billion seconds, which is the same as 50 million minutes, which is the same as 833,000 hours, which is the same as 34,000 days, which is about 95 years. [3,000,000,000 seconds ÷ 60 seconds per minute ÷ 60 minutes per hour ÷ 24 hours per day ÷ 365 days per year = 95.1294 years.] And remember, it would take that long only if you never stopped for a break! Good luck!

Since most of the numbers between one and one trillion are even larger than those on the way to one billion, the average time required to pronounce them is also longer. Try, for instance, 369,472,888,227 (three hundred sixty-nine billion, four hundred seventy-two million, eight hundred eighty-eight thousand, two hundred twenty-seven). How long did that take you? I would say that six seconds is an average time per number in counting to a trillion. (Remember, you have to pronounce every syllable!)

That means it would take six trillion seconds or 190,259 years to reach the number one trillion—assuming, of course, that modern science discovers the secret of immortality long before you achieve your goal. [6,000,000,000,000 seconds ÷ 60 seconds per minute ÷ 60 minutes per hour ÷ 24 hours per day ÷ 365 days per year = 190,259 years.]

GOLDFISH …

As a general rule, an aquarium should hold one gallon of water for every one-inch goldfish. That means that a million goldfish would require one million gallons of water. There are 7½ gallons in a cubic foot of water, and so one million gallons is equal to 133,333 cubic feet of water. [1,000,000 gallons ÷ 7.5 gallons per cubic foot = 133,333 cubic feet.]

A goldfish bowl approximates a sphere in shape. But it has been flattened at the bottom in order to have a surface that can rest on a table or shelf, and it would not be filled to the very top. So, while the volume of a sphere is calculated as $\frac{4}{3}\pi r^3$, we should assume that our fishbowl will hold somewhat less water—πr^3 would be a reasonable estimate. A bowl holding 133,333 cubic feet of water would thus have a radius of about 35 feet. [Trust me!] Since a sphere's diameter is twice its radius, the bowl would be 70 feet across. Adult whales of several species reach about 60 feet long, and so one of them would fit nicely into this fishbowl, although it wouldn't be happy there for very long.

A billion goldfish need one billion gallons of water, which is equal to about 133 million cubic feet. [1,000,000,000 gallons ÷ 7.5 gallons per cubic foot = 133,333,333 cubic feet.] In New Orleans, the Louisiana Superdome, one of America's newest stadiums, is 680 feet in diameter and 283 feet high.

Geometrically, a stadium is much like a cylinder, the volume of which is calculated as area of the base times height. The volume of the Superdome is thus about 102,724,000 cubic feet, which is quite close to the amount of water required for our fish. [The area of a circle is πr^2; in this case r, the radius of the circle formed by the base of the stadium, is 340 feet; π is approximately 3.14; the area of the base is thus calculated as 362,984 square feet. Multiplying this area by a height of 283 feet, we arrive at a volume of 102,724,472 cubic feet, slightly less than the 133 million cubic feet our billion goldfish would require.]

A trillion gallons approximates 133 billion cubic feet of water. [1,000,000,000,000 gallons ÷ 7.5 gallons per cubic foot = 133,333,333,333 cubic feet.] How much water is in a city harbor? It varies, of course, according to the city. But it would be reasonable to imagine a large natural harbor, semicircular in shape, extending seven miles inland, with an average depth of 50 feet. The volume of water in such a harbor would be about 100 billion cubic feet, approximately what's needed by our enormous school of goldfish. [Volume equals area times depth. Since this is a semicircle, the area is $\frac{1}{2}\pi r^2$; r = 7 miles × 5,280 feet per mile = 36,960 feet; area = $\frac{1}{2}$ × 3.14 × $(36,960)^2$ = about 2.14 billion square feet of water. The volume would then be approximately 2 billion × 50 = 100 billion cubic feet of water.]

TINY STARS …

The basic star pattern we have used contains 108 stars across by 133 stars down; 108 × 133 = 14,364 stars per page. Since there are seven pages, we would have 7 × 14,364 stars = 100,548 stars. That's more than 100,000 stars, even allowing for the size variations we've included.

As you have seen, one hundred thousand stars can be put on seven pages. One million is ten times as big as one hundred thousand, so we would need 10 × 7 pages = 70 pages to show one million stars.

Since a billion is a thousand million, it would take 1,000 × 70 pages = 70,000 pages to show a billion of these tiny stars. Seventy thousand 9-inch wide pages would stretch across 9.94 miles. [70,000 × 9 inches = 630,000 inches ÷ 12 inches per foot ÷ 5,280 feet per mile = 9.94 miles.]

Since a billion stars cover about 10 miles and a trillion is a thousand billion, a trillion of the same tiny stars would stretch 10,000 miles. As an example, the distance between Auckland, New Zealand, and New York City is 10,194 miles.

D.M.S.

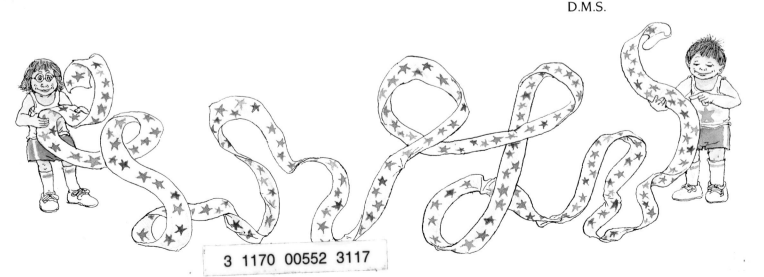